STICKY ICKY VICKY

Choosing to Be Myself

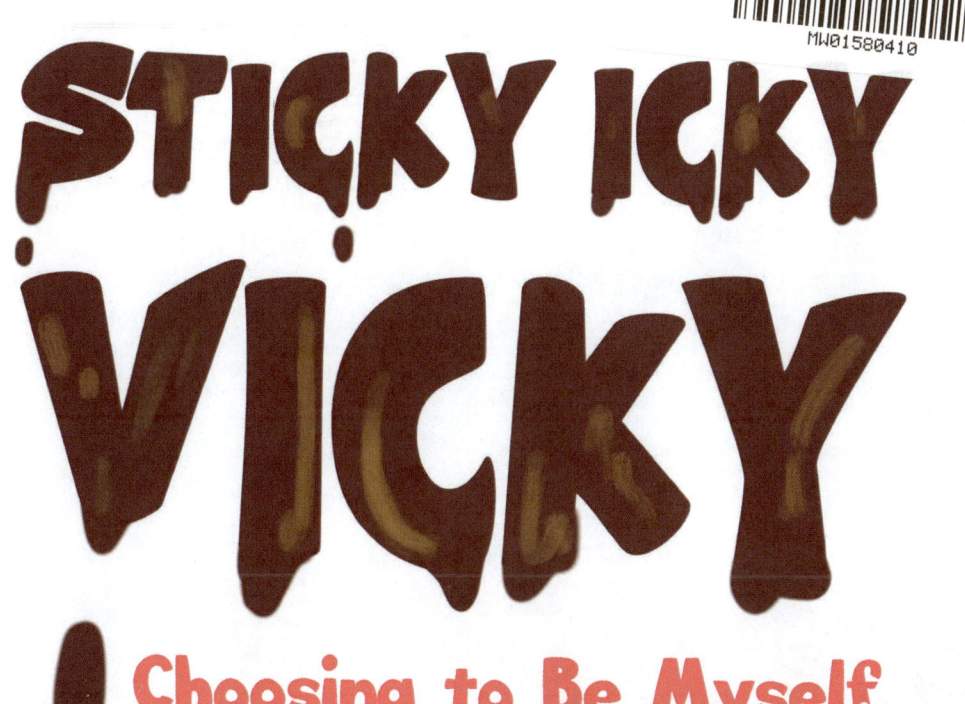

By Alysia & Michael Ssentamu
Illustrated by Noor Alshalabi

Copyright © 2022 Alysia Ssentamu and Michael Ssentamu

All rights reserved.
No part of this book may be reproduced, distributed or transmitted in any form or by any means, including photocopying, recording, or other electronic or mechanical methods without the prior written permission of the copyright owner except for the use of brief quotations embodied in book reviews and certain noncommercial uses permitted by copyright law. For more information, email: hello@stickyickyvicky.com

First Edition published 2022 by Pixel Publishing House

Cover, interior design and illustrations by Noor Alshalabi

ISBN 978-0-6451293-3-5 (paperback)
ISBN 978-0-6451293-4-2 (ebook)
ISBN 978-0-6451293-5-9 (audio book)

For more information about the authors, illustrator, book and for some amazing free resources please head to: www.stickyickyvicky.com

Publisher's Cataloging-in-Publication Data

provided by Five Rainbows Cataloging Services

Names: Ssentamu, Alysia, author. | Ssentamu, Michael, author. | Alshalabi, Noor Mohammad, illustrator.
Title: Sticky Icky Vicky : choosing to be myself / Alysia Ssentamu [and] Michael Ssentamu ; Noor Mohammad Alshalabi, illustrator.
Description: Mawson, AU : Pixel Publishing House, 2022. | Series: Sticky Icky Vicky. | Summary: Sticky Icky Vicky: Choosing to Be Myself tells the story of Vicky who must learn to embrace who she really is.
| Audience: Grades K-4.
Identifiers: ISBN 978-0-6451293-3-5 (paperback) | ISBN 978-0-6451293-4-2 (ebook) | ISBN 978-0-6451293-5-9 (audiobook)
Subjects: LCSH: Picture books for children. | CYAC: Bullying--Fiction. | Peer pressure--Fiction. | Self-esteem--Fiction. | Self-actualization (Psychology)--Fiction. | Girls--Fiction. | BISAC: JUVENILE FICTION / Social Themes / Bullying. | JUVENILE FICTION / Social Themes / Peer Pressure. | JUVENILE FICTION / Social Themes / Self-Esteem & Self-Reliance.
Classification: LCC PZ7.1.S84 Stc 2022 (print) | LCC PZ7.1.S84 (ebook) | DDC [E]--dc23.

This book is dedicated to our children, who are always challenging us and asking us hard questions (please ask some easy questions sometimes). You are all amazing and we love your ability to make us laugh as you learn and grow. We love you, because you are you.

TO ALL MY READERS, I hope you enjoy this book and find the courage to choose to be the real you, no matter what others may say or do.

Love from Sticky Icky Vicky.

VICKY is a delightful and kind, outdoor-loving girl,
with brown eyes and gorgeous hair with a curl.
She lives a stone's throw away from Crescent Moon beach.
With blue waters stretching as far as the eye can reach.

Vicky likes to play on the beach with best friends Rhea and Betty.
Jumping waves and flying box kites, getting sandy and sweaty.

But most of all, Vicky loves playing in her backyard mud pit.
Creating ways of getting dirty and absolutely loving it.

Vicky is often covered with dirt and mud from her head to her toes.
This is why people call her **STICKY ICKY VICKY** everywhere she goes.
Vicky adores her nickname, wearing her dirt-covered clothes with pride.
Getting muddy and dirty is something that Vicky has never had to hide.

One day, while playing with Rhea and Betty at the school playground, Vicky bumps Claire, who likes to tease and push people around.

"**Yuck,**" says Claire, frowning and pushing Vicky away.
"How can you come to school looking dirty every day?"
With tears in her eyes, Vicky says, "Stop being hurtful and mean."
Claire laughs and replies, "Dry your dirty, sticky tears, mud queen!"
"Hey Claire, stop your nasty behaviour," says Betty.
"Why are you picking on Vicky? It's mean and petty."

Vicky begins to doubt herself and her love for mud play.
What if Claire starts to tease her every single day?
So, Vicky decides to stop playing with all her friends outdoors.
Instead, she stays home looking sad, helping her mum with the chores.

"Why don't you go and play in your mud pit?" asks Vicky's mum.
"It may help cheer you up — you've been looking sad and glum."
"Not today, Mum," replies Vicky, "I don't feel like getting icky and sweaty.
I will help you in the kitchen instead. Let's cook some yummy spaghetti."

Vicky's fear of being teased sparks a voice in her head.
She calls this unhelpful inner voice, Negative Ned.
Negative Ned tells Vicky, "Stop getting dirty and stay clean.
If you get muddy, people will laugh at you and be mean."
He reminds Vicky of the pain of being bullied, teased and hurt.
Listening to Ned's voice is stopping Vicky from playing in the dirt.

One wet school day, the recess bell rings, and Rhea says to Vicky,
"Yay, it's time for messy fun at the playground! Let's go get icky!"
Vicky stands up from her desk with a strong urge to go play with her buddy,
but then sees Claire out the window at the playground trying not to get muddy.
All of a sudden, Negative Ned whispers softly in Vicky's ears,
"Don't go and get dirty, you will be teased and reduced to tears."

"Not now, Rhea," says Vicky timidly, "I will be bullied by Claire."
"Come on, Vicky," says Rhea, letting out a long sigh of despair.
"So what if Claire thinks your love of mud is strange?
You're perfect as you are, there is no need to change."
"Thanks," says Sticky Icky Vicky, sadly shaking her head.
"I don't want to get icky today. Let's go to the library instead."
"Okay," says Rhea, following Vicky into the school hallway.
"But we can't always go to the library, we need to go out and play!"

Suddenly, Vicky sees a crowd gathered at the notice board by the library hall. Each one of them is excitedly reading the new poster just pinned to the wall.

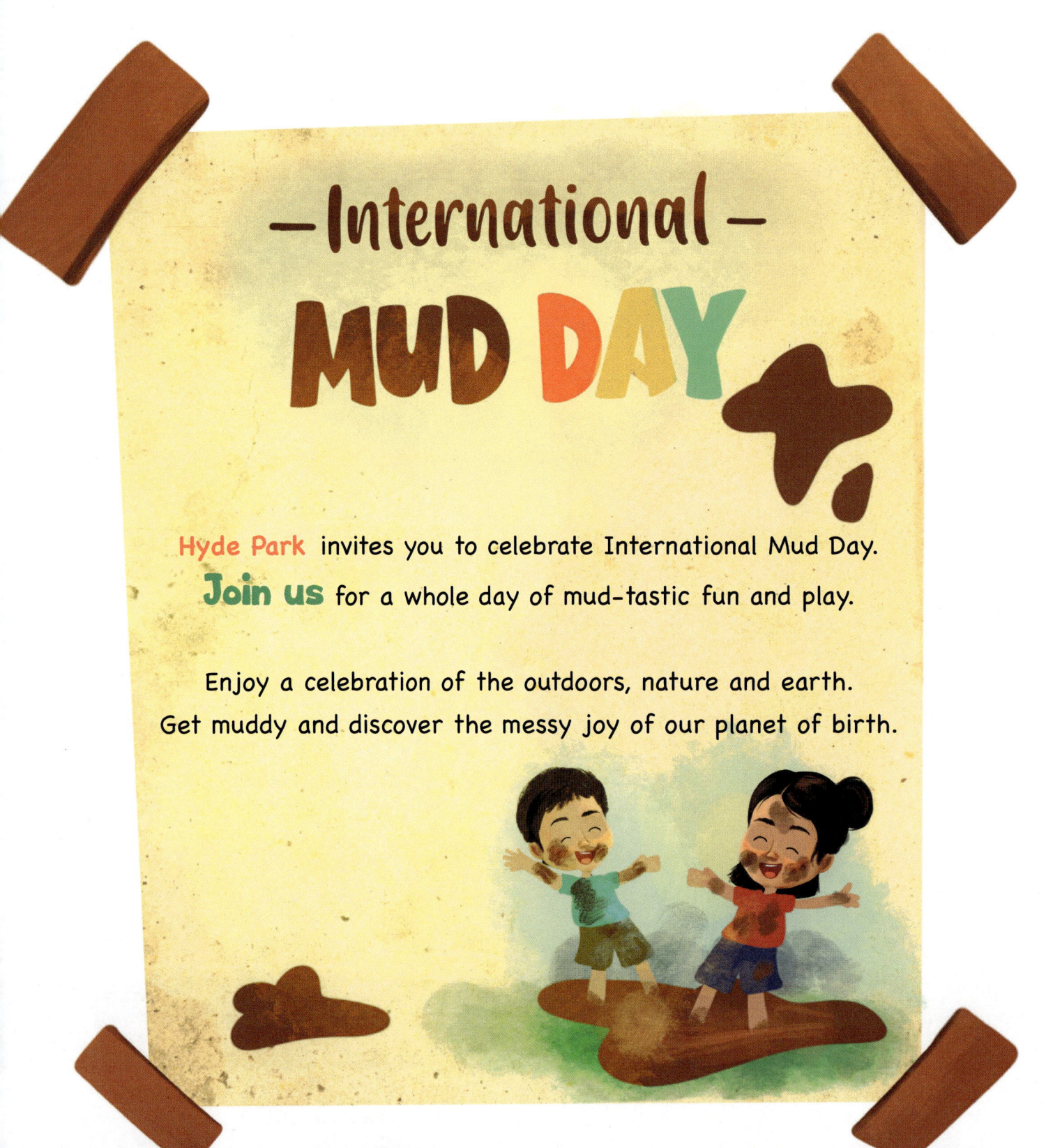

"What is International Mud Day?" asks Vicky, reading the poster with everyone.
"It's a mud festival celebrating nature at Hyde Park," says Rhea. "It's lots of fun!"
"You will love it," Rhea adds. "I would not miss it for anyone or anything."
Vicky imagines dancing in the mud with her friends and the joy that will bring.

Suddenly Ned pops into Vicky's head and says, "I wouldn't go to this mud show!"
"Why not?" asks Sticky Icky Vicky nervously. "I would really like to go."
"Everybody will be there, even Claire," replies Ned. "Are you mad?"
"I'm not mad," says Vicky, "but if I miss the Mud Day fun, I'll be sad.
There will be times when I'm muddy and will be teased and hurt.
What matters is that I choose to be brave and play in the dirt."
Determined to get back to being her true mud-loving self again,
Vicky stops paying attention to Negative Ned's voice in her brain.
She decides to go to the Mud Day festival, putting her courage to the test.
She knows being true to herself won't be easy, but she will do **her best.**

Hundreds of people turn up on International Mud Day the following Friday, all of them waiting patiently and happily for the start of the day's mud play.
Vicky arrives, excited and ready to play in the mud with everyone.
"Vicky," says Rhea, "remember, it's okay to be yourself and have fun."
"I will," replies Vicky happily, determined to show her friends she's no dud.
But then Vicky spots Claire standing next to one of the giant pools of mud!

"What's Claire doing here?" asks Vicky, fear creeping up her spine.
Betty smiles and says, "Come on, Vicky, be brave! You'll be fine."
"Hey Vicky," Claire calls out, "are you going to play in this cesspool?"
"Yes," says Vicky, determined not to let Claire ruin her day, "I think **it's cool.**
I can't keep pretending to be someone I am not, it doesn't feel right."
Vicky then pokes her toes into the mud and smiles with joy and delight.

The start whistle blows, and everyone jumps into the mud puddles.
Delighted to be icky again, Vicky gives her friends hugs and cuddles.
Watching in disgust, Claire starts to walk away, not wanting to get icky.
She takes a step, slips and falls awkwardly — into the mud **next to Vicky!**

"**Eek!**" screams Claire, feeling like a fool in front of her peers.
Vicky nervously helps Claire to her feet, despite all her fears.
"Ugh," cries Claire, trying to get the mud out of her hair.
"Why is everyone laughing?" she asks, looking around in despair.
"They are laughing because you slipped and fell in the mud," says Vicky.
"It is not nice being made fun of for getting dirty, icky and sticky."
"It does feel bad," admits Claire, ashamed to look Vicky in the eyes.
Claire's response to Vicky catches Vicky completely by surprise.
"Why don't you come play with my friends and me?" asks Vicky with a wide grin.
"Thanks," says Claire, but, though she is covered in mud, she isn't ready to join in.

Suddenly, Claire hugs Vicky and says, "I'm sorry I was **cruel** and **mean**."
"Thanks for apologising," says Vicky, "you're now the new mud queen.
Come on, let's play in the mud together and get all messy and sticky."
Claire decides to join Vicky, and for the first time has fun getting icky.

Vicky's courage sparks a new voice in her head.
She calls this helpful inner voice, Positive Ted.
Positive Ted tells Vicky, "Don't let others decide what is right for you.
It's okay to get dirty and play in the mud, like you love to do."
He reminds Vicky to always be who she really wants to be,
because her uniqueness is a strength, there for all to see.

Vicky is more confident, now that she listens to Positive Ted's voice.
She is getting icky and muddy again because she makes that choice.
"I have learnt to accept and love myself for who I really am," says Vicky.
"Someone's opinion of me doesn't decide how I feel or if I get to be icky."

Be proud of who you are and don't be ashamed to show people the real you. Love yourself and everything you stand for, it's the bravest thing you can do.

Use the statements and questions below to start a conversation about finding the courage to be yourself.

We have all heard the statement "just be yourself" — it sounds like an amazing thing to do, but sometimes this is easier said than done.

There are two versions of ourselves that we can be — our true self and our false self.

What does "being your true self" mean to you?

What does "being your false self" mean to you?

Being our true self means being true to our real feelings and desires. Our false self is a side of us that has changed our behaviours and feelings because of other people's judgments, labels and our desire to please others.

Do you know of any situation that has made you scared to show people the real you?

What is it?

Don't try to fit in with your peers and hide your true self out of fear of other people's opinions.

What do you think or believe people think about you?

What can you do if you feel you are not being your true self?

You can always talk to a trusted adult about your concerns.

Learn to accept yourself and be proud of who you are.

How do you see yourself?

A) What are your positive thoughts?

B) Do you have negative thoughts? What are they?

ABOUT THE AUTHORS

Michael and Alysia are authors of the award-winning Sticky Icky Vicky series, which also includes Sticky Icky Vicky: Courage over Fear.

They are husband and wife health professionals who firmly believe it isn't hoarding if your stuff is cool. They live in the Australian Capital, Canberra, with their children, a dog, an African grey parrot, tropical fish and some chickens.

ABOUT THE ILLUSTRATOR

Noor Alshalabi is a Jordan-based illustrator who started drawing ever since she learnt how to hold a pencil.

After getting her BA in Visual Arts and Design, she pursued her dream of turning her imagination into reality through children's books.
You can always find her with a cup of coffee, curled up with a good book, watching movies, playing with her pet bird, spending time with a friend, or going for a hike. Nature is both her source of inspiration and relaxation.

LISTEN TO THIS BOOK!

Scan the QR code or use the link provided for a free audio reading of this book.

https://bit.ly/choosingtobemyself

For any questions or to tell us what you think of the story, email us at
hello@stickyickyvicky.com

If you want to learn more about Sticky Icky Vicky and her journey, go to
www.stickyickyvicky.com

COLLECT MORE STICKY ICKY VICKY STORIES

Meet Sticky Icky Vicky, a girl who wants to get over her fear-once and for all.

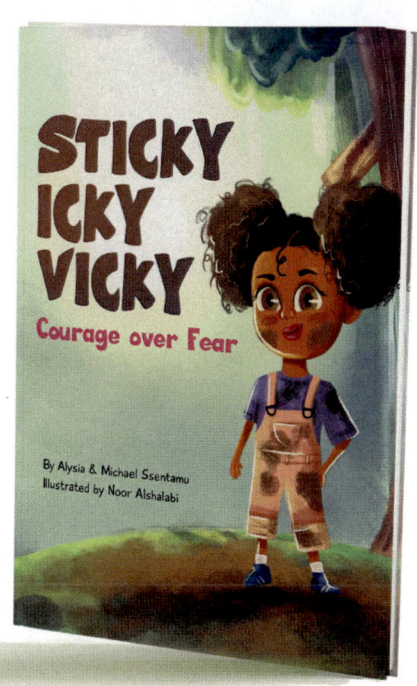

"An encouraging tale for young readers with their own fears to face."
- Kirkus Reviews (starred review)

We would like to thank you for your support. Without you, we would not be able to keep writing our beloved Sticky Icky Vicky tales. If you would like to help keep our dream alive, a review on Amazon would help us to spread the word. Much love from our family to yours.

Made in the USA
Middletown, DE
23 February 2023